THE LIBRARY OF CONTEMPORARY THOUGHT

America's most original voices
tackle today's most provocative issues

WALTER MOSLEY

WORKIN' ON THE CHAIN GANG
Shaking Off the Dead Hand of History

"Everywhere I look I see chains, from the planned obsolescence that binds us to an endless line of ever more useless machines to captivating television shows *about nothing* to the value of the dollar bills insecurely nestled at the bottom of my pocket. In America and elsewhere, race, gender, sexual preference, and even physical size lock us into roles that rarely come naturally. We are cinched into work schedules, production lines, codes of behavior, and timetables for personal advancement based on the array of the rest of our chains."

ALSO BY WALTER MOSLEY

Black Genius

Blue Light

Always Outnumbered, Always Outgunned

Gone Fishin'

A Little Yellow Dog

RL's Dream

Black Betty

White Butterfly

A Red Death

Devil in a Blue Dress

WORKIN' ON THE CHAIN GANG

Shaking Off the Dead Hand of History

WALTER MOSLEY

THE LIBRARY OF CONTEMPORARY THOUGHT
THE BALLANTINE PUBLISHING GROUP • NEW YORK

The Library of Contemporary Thought
Published by The Ballantine Publishing Group

Copyright © 2000 by Walter Mosley

www.randomhouse.com/BB/

Library of Congress Cataloging-in-Publication Data

Mosley, Walter.
Workin' on the chain gang : contemplating our chains at the
end of the millennium / Walter Mosley.—1st ed.
p. cm. — (The library of contemporary thought)
ISBN 0-345-43069-7 (alk. paper)
1. United States—Race relations—Forecasting.
2. United States—Social conditions—1980– —Forecasting.
3. Afro-Americans—Social conditions—1975– —Forecasting.
I. Title. II. Series.

E185.615.M645 2000
305.8'00973—dc21   99-016196

Text design by Holly Johnson

Manufactured in the United States of America

First Edition: January 2000

10   9   8   7   6   5   4   3

CHAPTER ONE

INTRODUCTION: AN OVERVIEW

1.

THE END OF THE CENTURY can be perceived as a border, a milestone, a marker for the human race that symbolizes, somehow, our tenacity. We've been slogging away at it for thousands of years and we're still here despite all pitfalls. In defiance of the elements, plagues, wars, madmen, and human nature itself, we are still striving, still trying to make sense of it all. We're still alive.

We're still dying too. Still suffering and killing and hating each other. We are well versed in the craft of diplomacy; this because we have become masters at the art of war. We have defeated the democratic process, living instead within an economic system that perverts our labor in order to create riches based on a sub-culture of poverty and crime, a system that any other creature would see (if she had our intelligent eyes) as barbaric.

We call ourselves the most advanced of all the

species but show very little understanding or respect for the bodies we inhabit or the world we
live in.

For over a hundred years the practice of slavery has been outlawed in the West. But people still
slave. Technology has taken us to the moon, but
not before it managed to eradicate millions of unwanted souls in the search for genetic purity; not
before our greatest technological project, harness-
ing the atom, reduced tens of thousands of men,
women, and children to shadows and dust.

THE CHANGE OF CENTURY AND millennium, we
hope, will allow us to forgive and forget this brutal
past. There is an overwhelming sense that a new
day will bring amnesty from all our failings. It is
as if after one big party and a twitch of the
chronometer we can start with a new slate—the
whole human race making resolutions for the new
millennium. No more cigarettes. Time to get in
shape. No more fooling around, no fooling, and
real honesty this time in following our religious
and moral convictions.

With all of this bright promise and emphasis

on the new and optimistic there are few who care to listen to commentary on the chains we're dragging out of the darkness and into the future. The chains we've inherited from our mother's mothers and our father's fathers, chains, like those of Dickens' Marley, that represent all of our misdeeds: the shackles of slavery, the restraints of capitalism, the corruption of idealistic systems, and the iron convictions of hatred, prejudice, and ignorance—these are our baggage.

These misdeeds are evidenced by the fact that today our powers and potentials are not equaled by our moral achievements. We have the power to end starvation, but the distended bellies of starving children around the world go unfilled. We celebrate the chemical cocktails that impede the progress of HIV, while at the same time that plague decimates much of the African continent. Our abilities far outmatch our actions. This is because our actions, and the actions taken in our names, are not truly ours to govern.

Decisions are made by governments in concert with corporations that are designed to increase profit and influence, not to advance humanitarian ends. Children are starving but that has nothing to do with business. People are dying but you can't try an international cartel for murder.

The lack of moral responsibility and leadership in the world is appalling. We know that something's wrong, but why don't we do something to change the way decisions are made? Because we've been shanghaied. We've been drugged and chained and made into property.

Television is our opium, our nightly bowl of hazy, unfocused dreaming. And money is the super-drug, the one fix that you can't leave cold turkey—because the withdrawal would be fatal. Money has also formed the bonds of our imprisonment. Our labor binds us to systems that can see us only as units of value or expense.

And so as the millennium envelops us our hopeful dreams are careening toward a wall of dread, dread that what might be coming will be worse than what has already come to pass for so many millions.

Our labor is designed to maintain the values of our economy. A stick of butter, an ounce of lead, a human life—each of these units conveys value in our world. Not human values but the values of the system that rules us. We drag along these values accepting the consequences: strategic wars, the laws that maintain order (and, subsequently, the police and prisons to enforce that order), heavy armaments, and the desire (the perceived need) for world dominance. This is the heavy curtain of chains that looms in our future.

Beyond the veil, we are told, there awaits a paradise. But we know that there will be an admission ticket and a closing time tacked on to that utopia. We will have to pay for our future every day. We'll pay in sweat and blood and sacrifice. The future may be bright, but we fear the majority of its citizens will be beasts of burden hauling around the fuel necessary to maintain the brilliance.

Nothing, it seems, can save the masses from this fate.

Nothing, that is, if we cannot free ourselves from those cold chains anchored in the crimes and ignorance of the past hundred and more years.

In order to free ourselves we cannot ignore our bonds, pretending that they don't exist as we have for so long. We must consider the nature of these chains. Understanding something of the process that forged these links might allow us the slack we need to slip away—carrying only our personal loads, our children and our humanity, toward their full potentials. Once freed, we might enter this new era realizing that the dreams we once had for a bright future were just dim hopes compared to the possibilities that lay dormant within us.

2.

I sat down to write this essay thinking that I was going to address race at the end of the twentieth century. Race, that heavy load on the mind of every black woman and man. Race, our defining characteristic. Race, which has forged all that is wonderful and terrible about America, its European *founders* and their victims.

I was going to write about the fallacy of celebrations based upon the multiples of ten-year anniversaries, pointing out that advancement is not defined by the passage of time but by deeds and change. To prove this argument I was going to contrast advancements in technology and technique with the change in our attitudes toward life and freedom, the former making strides forward that are no less than miraculous and the latter having changed very little—if at all.

It's pretty easy to prove this claim by juxtaposing the black struggle for freedom and equality since 1865 with advances in, let us say, transportation.

In 1865 the steam-driven train was the most advanced form of transport, while, at the same time, newly freed slaves were just beginning their experiments with freedom.

By the 1960s many African-Americans were still fighting for the right to vote, while techno-logical advancement had brought us into outer space. On one hand there is shamefully little advancement, while on the other there is more than one could have imagined.

This argument seemed to me a good reason for black Americans to resist the false celebrations and hopes of a new day grounded in a calendar-based notion of progress.

Black men, I wanted to argue, are not recipients of the promise of America. Instead they are underemployed and, too often, imprisoned. Black women are pressed to the extreme of their physical and emotional limits and then praised for their *strengths*.

But every time I sat down to write, the words seemed a bit too facile and rhetorical. The arguments were true enough but they didn't lead anywhere. The complaints and proofs against racism, as valid as they were, had no exit, no possibility for change.

Regardless of the poignancy of the crimes against black Americans our oppression is, after all, only a part of a much larger malignancy. The American structure of slavery was a consequence of the economy of the New World, its roots in Europe, not Africa. Mass oppression for mass production is a part of the Western psyche. Therefore the problems experienced by blacks in America have to be seen as part of that larger malady. It is impossible to extricate the black experience in America from the larger American experience.

The dogma of racism attempts to deny any solidarity that might exist between the races. For centuries racists (of all hues) have pointed out differences in culture, society, and even, they sometimes claim, genetics. These claims and superstitions have, for many years, kept the races apart. But as time has passed the races have been forced together by production lines, mass media, and grand social events, such as the civil rights movement, war, and the advent of popular music. The different races have become neighbors, co-workers, and cousins.

Where it was once easy to separate people of color from whites (by status in society, cultural differences, language, history, and lack of Anglo-European "sophistication"), we now find ourselves intertwined. Even if blacks and whites do not see—or do not want to admit—the similarities of their situations, those parallels still exist.

Class has a prominent role in the lives of *all*

Americans. Poor medical care, job insecurity, the bane of old age, lack of proper education, and that nagging sense of mistrust of a society in which you are a productive member who does not seem to share in the fruit of that production—these issues pervade every cultural group, creed, race, and religion.

The juggernaut of capitalism, having broken the bonds of its imprisonment—national borders—exacts its toll in an equal-opportunity manner. It is the nature of capitalism to apply its value system to everything. Within this system all values are interchangeable. Three ounces of gold, let us say, are equal in value to two and a half tons of sugar. A particular six-carat ruby might be equivalent to fifteen acres of arable land. One year of physical labor is (one hopes) equal to the resources it takes to keep that worker working for 260 out of 365 days.

Not only are these values interchangeable, but they also fluctuate according to market pressures. The cost of a barrel of crude oil, for example, might drop if new wells are discovered and exploited in some untapped part of the world. The ensuing competition in price could well affect the cost of production. One of the major production costs is labor. Therefore, the value of life itself fluctuates according to the cost of production.

The economic system, the system that rules so much of our lives, does not, probably *cannot,* value human labor above any other commodity or resource. Under the weight of this system a man's labor is no more valuable than its equivalent cost in pounds of potatoes.

In some ways this system further diminishes the specter of racism. You can't pull the computer aside and tell it some derogatory joke about Negroes or Jews. Capitalism has no race or nationality. Capitalism has no humanity. All that exists in the capitalist bible is the margin of profit, the market share, and those quirks of individualism that must be dealt with in much the same manner as a mechanic must deal with a faulty element: removal and replacement.

We are all part of an economic machine. Some of us are cogs, others ghosts, but it is the machine, not race or gender or even nationality, that drives us.

I'M NOT SAYING HERE THAT race is no longer an issue in America. Far from it. Race is one of the primary controls exerted over the lives of Americans. Blacks have been marginalized in this culture. The vestiges of four centuries of prejudice and psychological conditioning (added to skin color and other physical attributes) make it easy to single us out and demonize us. The lack of a true understanding of African-American history and its relation to the rest of the American story keeps the whole nation from a clear understanding and articulation of the present-day political and economic problems that face us all.

Black people are feared, hated, and blamed for all kinds of social maladies. And, having been culturally isolated for so long, we have also become celebrated curiosities who have maintained certain artistic traits that most of the white population can only mimic. Blues, jazz, rap, tap, slang, style, and that impenetrable visage put on to protect what little freedom of personality we have managed to maintain—these attributes represent a mountain of gold that others have mined and stolen.

Music and style in black America are so vibrant because they are barely veiled codes that express the pain we've experienced for so many years—pain that is common to *all* women and men, black and white.

The oppression of racism is a palpable part of life in America, so much so that the broader problems facing us today might have their solutions in understanding the opposition that African-Americans have put up against the system that has kept us down. Living on the fringes of production, we have been forced into an intimate relationship with the inequities and cold logic of America's value system.

You don't have to say "excuse me" to a slave. You don't need to cajole a people who are held in check by the fear of lynchings and privation. You don't have to sit across the negotiating table from a group that is landless, outnumbered, and outgunned.

What black people have experienced as a group for centuries many whites now experience as solitary and alienated individuals. In their various groups white Americans might feel that they belong, that there is a group spirit that looks out for them. But individually they suffer the barbs of bureaucratic indifference and the vicissitudes of corporate whims like everyone else. At the group level a white man might identify with the white, male, Christian president. But that identification means very little on the unemployment line or when the HMO refuses to supply possibly life-saving technology.

Every American is a unit of labor. That labor is possessed by an employer. Each individual may dispose of his or her labor as he or she wishes, but in most cases that work can be utilized only by the company that sells the ensuing product. The employer owes the laborer nothing. He may depend on our labor, but the advantage of supply and demand is in his favor, not ours. In a very real way this unites the historical experience of African-Americans and the new day dawning on the rest of the nation.

AND SO INSTEAD OF CONCENTRATING on the future effects of racism I am, in part, looking at race to provide a key to the problems that face all of us in America. I want to understand how we can free ourselves from the chains that define our range of motion and our ability to reach for the higher goals. These chains might be more recognizable in the black experience, but they restrain us all.

3.

A final note on the politics of this essay: I am not pressing forward with any extant ideology or dogma with these ideas. This is to say that I am not looking to the socialist or communist experiments of the twentieth century to answer our economic or social problems. Instead I want to look directly into the voracious maw of capitalism to see if there is a way to survive the onslaught.

Rebellion, I believe, is the primary movement in understanding. Violence and oppression rob us of the ability to understand. Without understanding, there can be no growth, no recognition of truth, and no tomorrow—only an endless repetition of gray todays.

In the pages that follow I will talk about the restraints placed on us by history, economics, self-image, the media, politics, and our misuse of technology and technique. These restraints are our chains.

Where it is appropriate I will use examples from the black American experience to underscore the nature of these bonds. But this is not a racial argument. Instead this is an attempt to address a series of problems and limits in our society that may seem insurmountable; these problems and limits face everyone in America, and therefore the dialogue concerns us all.

CHAPTER TWO

CHAIN, CHAIN, CHAIN . . .

EVERYWHERE I LOOK I SEE chains, from the planned obsolescence that binds us to an endless line of ever more useless machines to captivating television shows *about nothing* to the value of the dollar bills insecurely nestled at the bottom of my pocket. In America and elsewhere, race, gender, sexual preference, and even physical size lock us into roles that rarely come naturally. We are cinched into work schedules, production lines, codes of behavior, and timetables for personal advancement based on the array of the rest of our chains.

What we see in the media is censored, sometimes by religious groups and zealots but most often by the more efficient system of supply and demand. What we see is what sells: television shows that titillate, distract, or relax us, and commercials that charge us for being fooled.

The blending of the races in Los Angeles or America's halfhearted commitment to democracy around the world gets short shrift compared to spectacular murders and the sexual exploits of our political leaders.

We are hemmed in by expectations from both extremes. On one hand the images of the most beautiful, the most intelligent, the strongest, the bravest, and the most evil are shown twenty-four hours a day on TV shows, in movies, on magazine covers, and even in the news. Conversely, a child can make it all the way through high school without learning how to read properly. Most children get their early education with no deep knowledge of their history or culture.[1] This ignorance is a bond stronger than steel.

Not all chains are man-made. There are natural limits that every human throughout history has

---

[1] Here we see a connection between African America historically and contemporary American culture on the whole. Black Americans have been cut off from their history in two ways. The first was the loss of the memory of home (country of origin, history, language, and culture). The second loss has been the refusal of American historians to record and promulgate the contributions of blacks to this nation's history. Because of these blockades most African-Americans have missed the chance for a solid, uniting feeling of culture.

Today, however, most young Americans, regardless of race, have not been properly schooled in history and culture. Popular culture, to a great extent, has replaced the deeper variety.

had to contend with. The aging process, vulnerability to disease, failing eyesight, genetic traits, the sometimes uncontrollable urges of the instincts—all these are fundamental human limitations. Our intelligence and its ability to see beyond its capacity to understand make us all the more aware of these limits.

Death is the final link, of course, the eyebolt that holds fast all our other chains.

But even here, in intimate relation to our own bodies, we are further limited by the larger world. The medical industry makes a killing on the relief of symptoms and physical care. Our instincts are humiliated and then harnessed by codes of behavior. And how many times have you heard the phrase "I don't have to do anything but die and pay taxes"? Even death has a peer in the company store.

The process of freedom itself has been worked into the shape of fetters: White men in suits and ties, white women in suits too. Democrats and Republicans. Liberals and conservatives. Just left of center, just right of center. Keeping the status quo. The choices we are given in the political arena are almost completely dominated by the two major political parties. These parties are actually multi-million-dollar influence corporations that decide our issues based on their ability to raise money. Independents, radicals (left and right), and free-thinkers have no real voice in Congress or in the Oval Office. Democracy, to a great extent, has stopped being an ideal and a right. Today American democracy is a commodity ruled over by the monopolies of the Democratic and Republican parties.

MUCH OF OUR LIVES IS spent in various forms of restraint. Some of these restraints are the product of evolution (the relationship of the sexes, child rearing), some are social and cultural (laws maintaining order and protecting the rights of individuals), some are biological and genetic. But many limits, too many, are based on the orderly production of goods and the subsequent protection of the property of the wealthy.

Production and protection are always the jobs of the lower to lowest classes of society: peasants and their offspring, serfs and their brood, slaves and their children, both producers and property. The middle and upper classes enjoy the fruits of production while the worker strains to survive.

In ages past lords and their priests extracted pleasure while at the same time they controlled the spiritual consciousness of their slaves. This is our history. For centuries workers have slaved. For centuries organized religion has promised a better day after death.[2] But technology and technique in the modern age have shown promise for heaven right here on earth. All that we need in the way of food and shelter is available and possible for everyone. Not only is there the possibility for enough for all, but there is also the hope for exponential advancement.

Science, if it is nurtured and cultivated, can perform miracles that we can imagine no more than Robert E. Lee could have conceived of NASA and John Glenn's flights. We could extend life, extend youth, break the barrier of light.

Of course there are darker sides to science. The production of biological organisms for the purposes of warfare, bigger bombs dropped from higher heights, and stealth technology prove that science can be used against us. But even good

---

[2] "When you lay down your load," the preacher or priest would say, "then you can have eternal peace in the house of our Lord." This always seemed to me to be saying, "When I can't squeeze one more ounce of labor out of you, and only then, you can be free."

applications of technology can have their evil sides. The aforementioned plague of AIDS in Africa is going unchecked because the chemical technology needed to control it is too expensive to be practicable on that continent. Make no mistake about this unavailability. It is not something that is inevitable. It is a choice, a moral choice.

Advancements in science and technology are the crystallization of the potentials of the human race. Through these disciplines we can alter our fates and change our lives. To reduce these universal gains to a question of property creates a form of imprisonment that changes the golden sound of a choir of heavenly angels to a cacophony of the blues. When one can say that a capsule is worth more than a human life we know that the technology we create has become just another link in the chain.[3]

---

[3] One might say here that the refusal of the powers that be in America to help suffering Africans is a racial issue, that the same problem facing a *white* population would get an immediate response from our government and drug corporations. Certainly I believe that any group of people who are seen as a minority can more easily be ignored (i.e., the Jews in Nazi hands during World War II), but that doesn't mean that everyone else is protected. Any man, woman, or child, of any race, without power and wealth to back him or her up is likely to suffer the same fate as Africa. Poverty, not skin color, is the sin, and the key to the city of God is composed of property.

. . . CHAIN OF FOOLS

Of all the constraints placed upon us, <u>two of the most powerful</u> are those of spectacle and <u>illusion</u>. Chains are expensive, as are surveillance tools and armed guards. The best way to keep a worker working is to bedazzle her or him. Sublimation is the best remedy for rebellion. Give them something inconsequential to think about or a dream that leads nowhere.

Organized sports are perfect for these ends. Ferdinand Marcos distracted a whole revolutionary movement in the Philippines by hosting the Thrilla in Manila, the battle royal between Joe Frazier and Muhammad Ali.

Sports are good, sex is better. Movies, celebrations, mud-slinging elections, or a grisly string of murders (usually of socially expendable male or female prostitutes) can also be perfect for the derailment and subsequent pacification of the masses.

IMAGINE THREE MONTHS OF NO electronic or stadium distractions. What thoughts you might have. What things you might do—reading the newspaper[4] front to back (even better, reading a book), playing with the kids, examining your relationship with your spouse, long walks. Instead of watching the game, you meet your neighbors and play ball in the park. When the world is outside the door and your family is inside, certain forms might take shape. The center of your life might drift back into a form that includes *you* as someone who is important. And if during these months of media abstinence you limit alcohol intake to a drink or two a day, many doors of perception would open wide.

The pain experienced from such a sacrifice would be exquisite. All that time alone with your own thoughts. To give up the lies of the nightly magazine shows, the fantasies of professional sports, and the melodrama of the soaps would be harder than training for a marathon. To face one's own life, with all of its inadequacies, for twelve weeks— a great many Americans just could not do it. Psychologically it would be like the Outward Bound

---

[4] Even though newspapers are part of what I call spectacles and illusions, I hope that limiting the electronic (TV, movies, radio, etc.) and stadium (professional organized sports) events from one's life would give one enough leisure to question the information presented in a daily paper.

program that drops its clients in the middle of the wilderness with one directive: survive.

<u>There is a psychic wilderness that surrounds each of us, a wilderness of silence and self-evaluation that we spend most of our day avoiding.</u> Only in our sleep do we let go of the packaged spectacles. For most of us, <u>nighttime dreaming brings us closer to our identities and our power than any activity in the waking world.</u>

I'm not even asking that one give up TV and the Yankees. I'm just saying that one could *think* about it, that one might consider giving up the spectacles and illusions for ninety days. Of course, to do that one would have to concede that most of popular entertainment and so-called news is really an attempt (conscious or not) to distract us from thinking too much about the truth, about the reality of our lives. This is not a generally accepted fact in our society. The nightly news is important by definition. Popular films, once just bright lights and fluff at the end of the week, are now discussed as high art. The coronation of an English monarch has more weight than the execution of a poor mother's son. And that execution is more important than the fact that so many children learn almost nothing in public schools.

In the theater they call this phenomenon the

suspension of disbelief. We have accepted the blinding lights of popular culture as the true vision of our world. After all, aren't the movie stars and football players multimillionaires? Isn't that what we all really want to be?

If I didn't accept what was presented on TV as true, then where would I go to find the truth? If I didn't accept the electronic image's depiction of the world, how would I fit in at work and at the dinner table? Even if all the media told were lies, it would be difficult to ignore them because those lies are what everybody *else* believes. And so I would be alone with the silence and no closer to the true nature of things than I was when I was laughing at *Seinfeld*.

It's a hell of a lot easier to go along with the media and the desire to avoid what you suspect might be happening in the world. It is easier to get drunk and laugh at a sitcom or get fat and cry at a soap than it would be to sit in the stillness of your home with no distractions or lies. The chubby husband knows that he can't fit into his jeans anymore, but he still appreciates his wife's telling him that he's just as slim as he was back in high school. Sometimes a lie makes life more bearable.

The problem of finding the truth is further

complicated by the fact that discarding one set of illusions won't necessarily reveal a deeper understanding of the world. The prepackaged and glib representations presented by the media have no counterparts in the silence of your solitude. The world isn't waiting for you to see it; rather, it is waiting to be built by you and others. Those three months of solitude I suggested are the way to suspend the lies, but they are only the first step toward realizing your (our) potentials.

A NEW MOURNING

Considering that this essay is in part about the millennium and my proposition is that the strongest chains are of an illusory nature, I feel that a brief discussion of the celebrations that have attended, and will continue to attend, the thousand-year mark is warranted.

I've always been confused about the supposed importance of anniversaries; holidays, or commemorations of events based on the power of ten, are the ones most suspect. Fund-raisers know that you're more likely to gather interest on a fiftieth anniversary than on a forty-ninth or fifty-first. The two-hundredth anniversary of America's Declaration of Independence allowed the nation a celebration that lasted almost two years (this despite the fact that black men didn't obtain their freedom until almost a hundred years later than that declaration and that women, black and white, had to wait until the twentieth century for universal suffrage).

These celebrations, expectations, condolences, and times of reflection seem to me arbitrary, idle, and definitely consumerist. A good day to sell hot dogs and popcorn. A day to sell spectacles and hopes. A day to pretend that we can lay our bundles down and cross over to the other side, free from the grasping shackles of the past.

The baby born at midnight in the first time zone to cross us over into the next millennium will have been a magic baby, his or her photograph sold and shown all around the world. But in two years, when that baby's neighbor is dying from starvation, war wounds, or disease, no one will notice and no one will care, because death due to these all too regular occurrences is mundane. That death won't sell a newspaper or a TV ad, but a quirk of the clock will.

So when considering these big anniversaries, I usually end up thinking that even though we live in a very complex and technologically advanced world, we are just simple people, superstitious about numbers and colors and what our chances are to survive, looking at the big ball in Times Square while criminals pick our pockets, empty our bank accounts, and redefine the value of our labor.

If we have to recognize the passing of the millennium it would be more appropriate, I feel, to *mourn* the passage of that thousand years. A thousand years and genocide is still with us. A thousand years and children are still starving.

These are reasons to lament our failures, not to celebrate better days. And the truth is that many, many Americans agree with these sentiments. There's much that is wrong with our world. Even the upbeat news anchors on the major networks can't deny that. Something's wrong, wrong today. We don't have to wait one year or ten or a thousand to address the problems. Just go outside in any major city, walk a few blocks, and you will find someone down on his or her luck—way down. The human race's birthday means very little to one who is starving or dying.

If the new millennium deserves note, it should be in the form of a lament. We should, I believe, regret the passage of so many years during which we could have been moving forward. Instead of making resolutions, we should be making apologies to all the children starved and warped and made to settle for less because we were unable to see past the wreck of our own ancestors' failings.

THE CHAINS OF LOVE

This chapter has been meant to give a brief sketch of the limits placed upon us by our economic system and the diversions we have created in order to survive the privations imposed by those limits. From daily labor to political machines to the superior marketing of inferior products, not merely are we held back, we are also *defined* by the nature of these limitations. Not only is the political boss corrupt, not only do we realize that he is corrupt, but we still look to this person for guidance and leadership! We accept the terms of our imprisonment. We willingly participate in the lockdown of our humanity.

There are only two ways for the slave to deal with his master. The first is to deny the so-called master's right to own another human being, *any* human being. *I will not be controlled, I will not relinquish the right to exercise my inclinations, I will not serve without being served equally. And I will not accept this mistreatment of others.*

The second, and more common, way for the slave to deal with his master is to love him. *He, the bringer of pain, can also ease my suffering. He feeds me, tells me when I can take a break from straining over impossible labors. He has the power to set me free.*

When chains define the very nature of your humanity, they blend with your own image and you begin to love them as much as you love yourself. What you end up with is a love affair with your own imprisonment. Guards and wardens are seen as family and friends. A wife loves a battering husband. The black man basks in the warmth of white fantasies about his sexual prowess. White workers look at corporate domination of the rest of the world and say, "Hey, look at what *we're* doing."

This is what makes freedom so difficult. Freedom threatens this false love. Therefore freedom is dangerous; it could kill you. And freedom that seems synonymous with suicide doesn't come off as a panacea; it's more like Pandora's box. Who wants freedom when breaking chains feels like breaking your own bones?

What does freedom from obsession with the master and his chains feel like? It's like withdrawal from an addiction, like the death of your mother, like a knife in the gut. Our chains go beneath the skin, into bone. The inhalation of that first cigarette in the morning, that's a link. The smile on your face when you hear the theme song of your favorite TV sitcom, that's another. So is the satisfaction that comes when the candidate you voted for is elected. These feelings are good. Why would you want to question and examine what feels good? Because the feeling is an illusion. The cigarette is killing you, the sitcom is probably distracting you from potentials you may never realize, and that candidate will take your vote and sell it to the highest bidder.

TOWARD A NEW DAY

What you have read so far in this book has been simple to write. It's easy to complain. Sure, I can tell you that political and economic systems are evil and just as much enemies of human potential as the privations they supposedly protect us from. But what do I propose to put in their place? How can we change the structures that seem omnipotent, omnipresent, and omniscient? How can an individual (or the sum total of all individuals) stand against a partnership of structures that seem as inescapable as the certainty of death or taxes?

That's the hard part. That's the big question, the sixty-four-thousand-dollar interrogative. And, unfortunately, there will be no clear-cut answer forthcoming. This is because the definitive answer doesn't exist yet. As long as we are mesmerized by the spectacle of the world presented on TV and in newspapers, there will always be a system beyond our control. As long as we cannot think beyond the image created for us by the media and the selective memory of authorized history, we will live in gilded chains, our eyes blinded by electric images, our ears plugged into earphones. We see what we are shown, hear what we are told, are elated by the success of a nation that knows us primarily as the Social Security numbers that we could not decline.

EVEN THOUGH THE ANSWER TO this predicament is not yet obvious, there are questions, guides, approaches, and tools that we might make use of. I will attempt to present five brief approaches to some of the issues I've raised—the issues that I believe must be solved in order to free us from chains of the past:

- The black experience in America as a torch in the darkness
- The truth as a commodity and barometer for our own commitment to growth
- The man in the mirror
- Defining the great enemy—the margin of profit
- My platform for the presidency

I hope these different contemplations on liberation will stimulate some thoughts about what might be in everyday life. Rather than answers, they are departure points meant to ignite the creation of a new world, at least in the mind of the thinker (you). This new world is a dream, but it is no illusion. It will be the possibility of a future that includes a self unencumbered by chains of oppression. We will always have the limits of our humanity, but maybe we can slough off the chains of the slave masters.

CHAPTER THREE

A Torch in the Darkness

1.

BLACK AMERICANS HAVE EXPERIENCED CHAINS from day one in the New World. We were clapped into irons in the belly of a slave ship, sold, and then chained again on farms and plantations (both north and south), made to toil in fields that we would never enjoy the fruit of, bearing children who were first and foremost the property of the master, doomed to misery and disease and a short life devoid of history, respect, or any possibility of release.

That was the first few hundred years.

After that came what the government called freedom. From the plantation in chains to the plantation without chains, from working the plantation owner's land to sharecropping his land, from the slave laws to Jim Crow laws, from the slave master's whip to the Klansman's noose—this was freedom.

As bad as it sounds, as bad as it was, this was a great step forward. Freedom of physical motion, no matter how proscribed by property and Afrophobia, was a sweet nectar and a balm for all those centuries under lock and key.

We had freedom. We had obtained the dream. We were paid for our labor, given money that we could dispose of by buying books and whiskey and shelter for children whom we were free to raise. We could afford vanity and the right to congregate and to praise God.

But no matter the sweetness, freedom for the ex-slave had a bad aftertaste. Groups of white men appeared now and then to burn or brutalize. Our constitutional rights seemed up to a broad range of interpretations by white judges and elected officials. Our property could be confiscated (stolen) with little recourse in the chambers of the law. Women were raped. Men were murdered for the tone in their voice or the look in their eyes. Laws limiting our freedom sprang up around us, reintroducing chains into the lives of the freed slave. There were segregated toilets, lynchings that went unpunished, and life that was always entered through the back door. In these first few moments of freedom the seeds were sown for a century of inferior education and gerrymandered voting districts that made the few blacks who could vote powerless.

The novelty of faux freedom began to wear off with the second generation of liberated blacks. The obvious inequities tore at our self-image and our dreams. We came to realize (under pressure) that freedom is not a stagnant state but an ongoing process of growth that, if not allowed to flourish, becomes malignant.

The promise was not kept. Black people were denied the full range of freedom that the Constitution espoused. They were relegated to the most naked and brutal tyranny of capitalism. This experience became a chink in the shining armor of America. It created a group of people who were wholly dissatisfied with their lot, not because of the experience of poverty, but because there was no vision of a future in which they could see themselves prosper.

With no history other than slavery and no future because the white world blocked the way, black people never bought the American dream— at least not completely, at least not for long. The story of the history between blacks and whites was punctuated with lynchings and random violence. The accepted dialogue between the races was a partial return to the master-slave dynamic. Monetary and professional progress for blacks was generally an impossibility until far into the twentieth century.

The bonds of slavery were not that easy to break. Centuries of bondage couldn't be dropped overnight, or in a hundred years. The problem was further exacerbated by the fact that American history is based on the institutions of slavery, genocide, and theft. The indentured servants, the Indians, and the social incorrigibles, along with Africans, were forced to strain and die for the landed white male's dream of freedom.

Over hundreds of years, black people developed identities designed to deal with the tyranny of capitalism in its most naked state: slavery. We survived by absorbing unimaginable acres of pain into a collective unconscious that cannot forget. We submitted the words of the Christian God to memory and created the music that moves a world to sing His praises. We took that same music and spread it to the loamy earth with blues that rivaled Shakespeare and Sophocles in the articulation of human tragedy. We learned the dark avenues of the night where the trappings of one life could be shed and another donned, moving beyond the perception and understanding of white restrictions.

We found hope where none was given. We found food and clothing and laughter where others saw nothing left.

You got to be ready to move on, son, the loving father tells his boy. Maybe that child just landed a good job in the slaughterhouse or in a big hotel on one of the few paved streets downtown. He's just had his first payday and he's feeling pretty cocky. But he hears his father. He knows that nothing has changed and that nothing ever will. One day the boss might have a toothache and fire him out of spite. One day a dollar might go missing or a banister unpolished, and that will be the end of his good job, even if he worked there for twenty years. One day he might look twice at a white woman's figure and be killed before he can be fired.

Everything I own is in this bag of skin, the same blues-keen father tells his son. *And if I'm not careful, they might start takin' stuff outta there.*

These lessons, and hundreds more, have been passed down over the centuries. They are the secrets of survival meant to help you keep your head above water when the flood comes and you are encumbered in permanent chains.

These secrets were often spoken out loud, in earshot of the white boss, like the old slave calls that were also secret codes the field slaves used to pass news among themselves. Those calls often used sexual and religious metaphors to hide their meaning. The mention of the "sweet hereafter" might be a desperate bid for freedom; "getting satisfaction" might refer to escape or revenge.

Words spoken, even today, carry messages that go unheeded by those not in the know. Even repeating words first spoken by white people can sometimes result in a secret message.

Learn to read, the white adviser tells his student or mentee, meaning that reading will open up new worlds of possibility, that the knowledge needed for success and happiness will, in part, depend on this skill.

Learn to read, the black mother repeats to her son or daughter. But in the timbre of her voice you might, if you knew how to listen, hear a tone that is a little too proud to be a plea, that adds, *because that will help to protect you from the continual attacks you will get from the white man's world. Reading will get you to understand how much he has already destroyed you and how much more devilment he's likely to accomplish if you don't watch out.*

Black folks have learned to love inside a shell of hatred. *Is this self-hatred or someone else hating me?* There is no answer to this question. The source of loathing is indistinguishable from external and internal origins. For centuries the media have represented blacks in two primary ways: as negative images and as absence. Either we are shown as criminals, fools, peons, and victims, or we simply don't exist. This nonexistence occurs when images of venerated people—heroes, political leaders, bank presidents—and beautiful people are exhibited. These images have been reserved by whites for themselves.[5]

The deprecation of the black race is in the minds and culture of the white world, but it also resides in the minds of blacks. We hate ourselves for being victims, for not living up to the expectations designed to see us fail, for wanting to live where we are not wanted. Racism is in our language, our schools, our history, our popular culture, and in the dreams of success we are given by our most esteemed thinkers.

How can you love yourself while being despised and, at the same time, being taught self-hatred? Simple: You accept the images given and love them anyway. The love is not pure, maybe,

---

[5] In the past thirty to forty years these limits have begun to change. But the change is nowhere near complete, and the memory of our race is older than the minds that remember.

not completely at home in your mind, but it is love still and all, and it is powerful too.

We love our features, our foibles, and the unique way in which we hold off oblivion. This love is ecstatic and ambivalent. This love takes away as it gives. This kind of love is anchored in the truth and the tragedy of the blues; it is incomprehensible and yet unassailable. This kind of love knows no master. We might not remember Africa, but at least we know that we've forgotten something; at least we know that it wasn't always like this.

2.

Black American history is often presented in contradistinction to general (white) American history. Blacks are too often shown as anomalous victims in an otherwise brilliant and positive pageant of democracy and Yankee know-how.

Slavery, Jim Crow, and prejudice are issues we want to sweep under a carpet down in Mississippi somewhere. *It's those crackers,* one imagines the history book would like to say, or *It was the ignorance of a long time ago, but all that's over now.*

This desire to deny and marginalize the black

American experience does harm to every stratum of our society. To begin with, the black American experience is not an aberration. Native Americans were slaughtered for their lands. Landless citizens (in spite of their white skin) along with all women were denied the right to vote for many years. Homosexuality is still a *black mark* against many of our citizens. The South itself, a whole geographic region of the American dream, was blasted into poverty by the Civil War. That poverty lingered into the middle of the twentieth century.

The black American experience *is* the history of America. Our struggle to survive in the face of blinding hatred is in part a key to understanding how the chains forged in the modern world might be slipped and avoided in the future.

The black race has learned, the hard way, what white Americans are only just beginning to understand: not to believe the promises of politicians and corporate leaders. We've been hearing those lies for over a hundred years. We take the media with a pinch of salt, and we know that the most important part of the word retirement is *tire*, because getting old just means you're going to get exhausted making ends meet.

All those years when America was imposing its economic hegemony on the rest of the world, the middle-class (mostly white) population got along well. Job security and low inflation rates were the results of poverty in *other* countries, which couldn't compete with our advanced industrialization (and our armed forces). Fifty-three years ago, when World War II ended, a period of fat descended on the middle class. Poor people still suffered. Black poor people suffered more because there were few avenues for us to rise above the level of manual labor. And so we kept the memories of survival alive while others began to have confidence in the value of the dollar and the fact of perpetual labor. While others looked forward to cushy retirement and brighter tomorrows, the ghettos were studying survival and revolution.

These studies can benefit almost everyone today.

I DON'T BELIEVE THAT WHITE attention to black history should be couched in contrite guilt. Our history is a subject just like any other taught in school. In this study one should learn from the pitfalls and advances. White America (and yellow and red and brown America too) should look at the black experience as a method for all of us to overcome the weight placed on us by those systems that control the realization of our labor. The state of slavery, the aftermath of slavery, the fight for equality—these are the lessons to be learned.

The problem facing Americans today does not originate from racial conflict. The problem is the enslavement of a whole nation to the rather small and insignificant goals of the few who own (or control) almost everything. Black people have been warring against this type of injustice since we were brought here. Now almost everybody is in the same boat.

Black American history, I say again, is American history. There is an echo of Jim Crow in the HMO: people shunted aside, denied access, and allowed to suffer with no real democratic recourse. Downsizing is an excellent way of robbing a hard worker of her accrued wealth. The widening gap between rich and poor is a way of demonizing the latter, because poverty is a sin in the richest country in the world. These new systems of injustice wear the trappings of freedom, but they are just as unacceptable as their forebears. The only difference is that under these systems we all suffer. This time everyone is a potential victim.

Today's corporate leaders, today's owners of property, are the descendants (either figuratively or actually) of the men who owned plantations and slaves. Not only did they inherit the property and the wealth, but they were also bequeathed the methods of extracting riches from the labor of the masses: *Give her as little as you can, just enough for her to survive and slave.* This is the similarity. But there are differences too. Today the neoslave is made to carry her own chains to and from the job. She has to clothe herself and feed herself, look after her own health, and make sure she's on time. She must look after her own old-age pension, and even arrange her own funeral. In return she is paid a salary, which she can dispose of in any way she pleases.

But she doesn't set the prices on goods; she doesn't devalue the dollars that never seem to stretch far enough. She makes the inferior products that always need replacing (she might even be a designer of these commodities), but that is not her decision.

"Unfair," the owner of the production process says. "I am only another victim of the unpredictable changes of the open market. What I do I have to do. There is no possibility for me to go against the tide."

And he's right. The plantation owner of old

couldn't stay in business were he to divest himself of slaves. Slaves were the engines of production. But this argument has no moral weight. The stinking corpse of injustice cannot be deodorized by an excuse.

Today the worker is not only the engine of production but also the consumer. She sells her labor cheap and buys at full price.

The corporate leader is just another citizen, just another man. But that puppy has found the teat to suckle, while his brothers and sisters can only gnaw on each other's tails.

The corporate leader says that he can do nothing, that he's locked into the continual competitive wars of capital, forces far larger than any single man. He's like the man in *The Grapes of Wrath,* the man on the tractor who is about to level the Joads' house in Oklahoma. *It's not me,* the driver says. *It's the bank.*

My answer to this lame excuse is, *Then step aside. It's you who is tearing down my house, and that takes away your innocence.*

This is what all Americans need to say. *Stand aside. I will not accept your inferior products, your half-hearted health care, your apologies for my unemployment after twenty-two years without a sick day. I built*

America, one needs to say and to remember, *as did my ancestors. And America owes me something. I am here to call that debt due.*

White America over the past fifty years or so has been lulled into believing in a kind of emotional and monetary self-determinism. *I pay my own way,* this attitude proclaims. And it was true for a long time. For a long time America dominated the world market and brought home a few orts for the worker. But today's corporations carry many passports. They play one people against the other now. They are not beholden to the American worker. The workers' union has been rendered as anachronistic as a pinball machine.[6]

Whites, blacks, and all other groups face the same problems today. The income ceiling placed on Social Security recipients, homelessness among mothers and their children, being three paychecks from poverty, and the phenomenon of the working poor: These realities lie ahead in the bleak landscape of many Americans' new millennium.

Because of the false promises that the majority of Americans grew up believing in, there is little

---

[6] Now that corporations can move their industries to another state or another part of the world, the teeth have been taken from the union's bite. Unions are local, regional, and national, but big business has the whole world for a game board.

that prepares them to confront the debilitating forces that beleaguer their bank accounts and feelings of self-worth. There were the hippie and antiwar movements of the sixties. There was rock and roll (a black thing, really). But these stances were, on the whole, single-note complaints or dreams and therefore not very useful for the problems of today. Today we need organization that helps us to articulate our issues and change the world.

Malcolm X and the Black Panthers are good areas of study. *The Fire Next Time,* by James Baldwin, and the speeches of Martin Luther King Jr. will enlighten any ear willing to listen. A real understanding of the strategies of the civil rights movement would change the landscape of resistance in America today. And make no mistake: We *all* need to resist if we want to survive intact.

The black American experience is a subject that is supremely American. It is the history of a centuries-long war in which one group of people strove for justice, for a fair share. Relegating black history to an elective or a ghetto or a moment in the past holds us all back. Black history is a torch that can lead us out from the darkness. In order to find the way, we have to work together and follow one another's strengths.

Black history can't address every issue, but it can certainly talk about refusing to go another step without an accounting. It can show you how each man, woman, and child can be an impediment to injustice.

CHAPTER FOUR

THE TRUTH

1.

THE POLITICAL AND ECONOMIC LINKS of our bonds are important to deal with—but they are not everything. Our hearts and minds are also prisoners of the modern world. We live mostly in the closet, to borrow a term from the gay community. Our true natures are hidden not only from the prying eyes of the outside world but even from ourselves. We have notions and hints of who we are, but we cover up quickly and close our eyes because our sense of survival relies on a certain code of behavior and a need to feel anonymous.

This anonymity is important because if the truth got out, who knows what might happen? I could get fired, banned from church, ostracized by my friends. The truth out of your mouth could humiliate you, let everyone else know that you've lied for all these years.

Lying is great material for chains. Lies stick with you and multiply as life goes on, like viruses. Lies, after being told long enough, become similar to truth. I once asked a Russian friend what living in communist Russia had been like. "It's like this," he told me. "You are in a factory that has no windows. You know that the sun is shining outside, but there are loudspeakers in the walls that keep telling you that it is raining outside. Raining, raining, raining. You *know* that the sun is shining," he said, pointing in my face, "but still they say it is rain. For years and years they say it is rain. Until finally you give in and say to yourself, why would they lie?"

People lie to be kind, to make life easier for themselves, to seem important, to protect the people they love. People lie because they see so much possibility in a loved one who has made a few mistakes, or because they are told lies and repeat them honestly, believing that they are speaking the truth.

Little exaggerations on the résumé, allowing someone else to believe a false assumption they have about you, taking credit when you were not responsible—these kinds of lies are the fabric of everyday life, as inescapable as rain. These personal fibs are mostly harmless, usually acceptable forms of everyday discourse. The only reason even to mention them is that they lead to a broader system of fabrications.

Professional news providers lie too: newspapers, the nightly report on TV, twenty-four-hour radio news. In America the most important form of news-lying is simply leaving things out. We know everything about the activities in the Oval Office but are told almost nothing about the ten thousand kidnapped children forced to prostitute themselves and make war in northern Uganda. We know how much money every armed bandit has stolen from banks but almost nothing about how much the banks have stolen from us. We are told, during the commercial, how much some piece of clothing costs, but the returning anchor refrains from telling us what economic havoc we have caused in the third world by paying slave wages to local workers to make the price attractive.

Lies: Supercool cigarettes will make women leave their boyfriends and husbands for your embrace. We went to war in the Persian Gulf to protect the rights of the sovereign Kuwaiti state. There will always be poor people suffering and wandering in the darkness.

The producer of the nightly news will tell you that telling the truth will only end up in a canceled news program. No one will listen. No one will tune in. *News*, this professional liar will tell you, *is entertainment. It is paid for by commercials and listened to by people who want, more than anything else, to feel secure in their beliefs and their world. A little hard news about immediate issues, a little sports, some sex if possible, the antics of a slack-brained movie star or pop singer of the moment, and we're outta here.*

The truth is withheld to protect those who are afraid to know and also to guard the interests of those who own the arteries of information.

We are complicit in this duplicity, but, we ask, what can we do? Sure, the world is full of liars and lies, but what difference does it make? And even if it does make a difference, what can I do about it? I'm just one person trying to make it, trying to pay my rent and feed my kids. If a lie buys security, then I'm happy to play along.

This is a very good argument. The lie that makes things right, I believe, *should* be told. "He went that way!" you lie to the pursuing toughs when they are chasing down your brother. Good. Right. To tell the truth in this case would be wrong.

Would that most lies were so simple. What about the woman who smiles flatteringly at a man she despises, only because he holds the decision about her promotion in his hands? What about the black man who nods in agreement with his conservative white boss who says that Negroes have created their own problems?

These lies diminish the tellers. They imprison us in images, both internal and external, that make us what we hate. Is self-hatred worth the promotion? This is a good question too. As a matter of fact, it might be the most important question in our private lives. Should we make our hearts and minds into lies in order to get over? In order to serve?

What about your daughter, the young girl who sees you grinning like a fool at a man who is awful? Should she also swallow her pride one day? Should she give in to his pressure? How far will she go with the charade?

Lies make friends with one another while the people who tell these lies hate one another. This is the contradiction we live with. We bind ourselves in ways that will never allow our true emotions and potentials to surface. We live wearing masks.

2.

The overwhelming necessity of lying and the inordinate repercussions of telling the truth present a predicament that is unacceptable. We cannot live like this, but then again there seems to be no alternative. After all, an outpouring of truth could destroy good marriages, wreck friendships, throw families into poverty, even topple nations.

These are fantastic notions but not, I contend, hyperbole. The truth is stronger than any antibiotic or antiviral we know; sometimes it is a form of chemotherapy that, while curing the patient of the disease, kills him in the process.

As dangerous as it is, this tool, the truth, can be a step toward our liberation in the next millennium.

The truth, the whole truth, is unbearable. Remarking on how fat your mother is may not be necessary. Neither would telling a friend how stupid his child seems to be. You might refrain from making a public announcement about how much you don't like people who are different from you. A child who believes that she is stronger than her daddy doesn't need to be set straight. An old pair of eyes looking back on a love that may have never existed doesn't need more light.

But the truth does have a purpose. Telling the truth allows others to see who we really are, makes them treat us according to our declarations, and, therefore, places us in a position closer to our emotions. Telling the truth will open dialogues. Sometimes people will argue with your truth. Sometimes it will bring you attention, wanted or unwanted.

But the main effect of truth telling is that it will interrupt the flow of lies. It will cause small rents in the fabric of our incarceration.

Truths: I love you. I have always been afraid of women. I believe that life itself is some kind of conspiracy. If all matter vibrates, then everything is music.

It doesn't matter how wild or mundane the truth is. What matters is that you believe in something and are willing to say so.

One truth is a step toward freedom. Another truth is one more step. As a matter of fact, if one were to tell the truth once a day, I believe that the darkness that lies tend to cause would stop its progress in the life of that individual.

Your advances are uncalled for and I do not appreciate them, you tell your harassing boss on September 14, 2000. September 15 will truly be a new day.

Your ability to understand the ramifications that attend a policy decision is far greater than mine, you tell a competitor in the office. You've both learned from that interaction.

Life is sacred.

Truth is a powerful agent. It only needs to be

spoken once. After that the world has changed. So if one were to tell the truth once a day, then once a day a change would be wrought. It wouldn't have to be a holiday or the first day of a new millennium. It could be a chilly Wednesday in March. It could be over coffee at ten-fifteen.

Telling the truth (a *new* truth) once a day would be a rigorous exercise. But it might be worth the attempt. You don't have to tell everything. Others don't have to suffer for your freedom. But you could tell about something you love, something you need changed, something you imagine might be true. These words brought into the world will change things, of that you can be sure.

You may be wrong. You may get into trouble now and then. Growing pains are to be expected in healthy organisms. And in the long run, growth is good for all of us.

CHAPTER FIVE

THE MAN IN THE
MIRROR

"**I** SAW A BLACK MAN GOING into your house this morning, Joe."

"You did?" Joe might answer. "What was he like?"

This for me would be the ideal interchange: a dialogue in which a truth is revealed not because of the prescribed one truth a day but from honest inquiry.

How was the man dressed? What were his manners like? How old was he, and what was his ancestry?

Was he truly black, like some skin we've seen? Or was it a shade of brown tinged by orange or red or yellow?

Back in the real world, however, the information does not change. It was a man. He was black. That's all that's important, but there is a mountain of prejudicial information that lies beneath the surface.

Maybe Joe's wife was in that house. Maybe

Joe's life savings were squirreled away under the floorboards. Maybe, if Joe is a white man, this is a crime simply by the nature of the slim piece of information we have: A black man went into his house.

What Joe and his friend don't know could fill volumes. Ignorance informs their hearts. And the chains of ignorance are virtually unbreakable.

Jamal sees a white man approaching him. So do Chin and José. What do they see?

Who knows?

We are conditioned to make assumptions based on gender, race, and age. Often we don't see the actual man but only what he represents. A short skirt seems to say more about a woman than the book under her arm. Dirty hands say more about a stranger than the neatly sewn seams of his work pants.

We are bombarded with these prejudicial assumptions in literature (good and bad), radio, and bad jokes—TV and movies and political campaigns too. Our human-resources professionals have these failings, as do our parole boards and colleges and elementary schools.

A stutterer or someone under three feet tall, any person with a Spanish accent—these people are, too often, well known before they can be known at all. Our assumptions about intelligence, morality, disease, and potentials for evil are right out of the can, ready-made. It's no wonder that our moral intelligence has progressed so slowly over the millennia. We very rarely use our eyes and ears for more than watching television repeats or listening to golden oldies.

Yes, it was a black man walking into Joe's house. What does that mean? Even imagining the worst, Joe is still faced with a unique event that will take time to understand and resolve. What was the man's name? What unique qualities did he possess? How did this man find his way to Joe's front door? Why is Joe, or his friend, so upset about the prospect of a Negro at his doorstep? Would a white woman be less intimidating?

If you can't question the world around you, seeking real answers, then you are trapped by the false answers provided by prejudice. And if you can't question your own assumptions, then you are not going to fit into this century very well. As a matter of fact, you didn't fit into the previous century any better. Because if science has taught us anything, it is that we must always be ready to question our assumptions. Otherwise we are trapped by ideas that will betray us and sabotage our potentials for advancement.

Sounds dramatic, I know. But we are social creatures. That is, we associate with each other because this association promotes our ability to survive. We take actions as groups and as individuals to ensure this survival. These actions are meant to produce safety, shelter, sustenance, and growth. A misstep will end up in a fall. A lie will lead to a dry pond. A mirage will bring us to a patch of arid desert and leave us there to die.

In order to be free to profit from the association of other people, we must look more closely at the world we live in and at the people in that world. A close look will reveal truths enough to tell for weeks on end. The richness and variety in each man and woman are so vast that you could consider the nature of one individual for weeks. You might not like this person, but most likely that will not have much to do with their genitalia or the color of their skin.

A STRANGER MIGHT TAKE A whole month for you to understand. Understanding yourself, behind the facades grown over the decades, will take a lifetime. *You* are the greatest assumption. Every nerve ending and length of chain is so close that they are difficult for you to discern.

Even understanding how one sees others (such as Joe's friend and the alleged black man) depends upon the image in the mirror. Who is that guy?

What do you see when you look in the mirror? A face aging over time, deepening almost imperceptibly? Someone familiar or maybe strange and new? You see a mood of the moment, or maybe you remember a thought from another time when you gazed at that same face. You see your eyes, windows in the glass.

Maybe sometimes you see a gender or an age, a race or ethnicity that you are identified with.

Sometimes you see yourself, a kind of totality of experience and memory. Everything you ever were or hoped to be, even those things that you have forgotten, is staring back at you. You. Beyond a name or race or gender. The center of an identity. Welcomed, loved, maybe even hated—maybe a failure. A you that can be moved and manipulated as if by magic through thought, widening the eyes, smiling, or giving a sincere look deep into the eyes that you know best. A you that cannot be changed, who has followed a crazy path to this very moment without cease, maybe without control. The aging that cannot be halted. The life lived that cannot be withdrawn. Every sin and good deed awaiting judgment.

Now and then you might see your mother or brother in that gaze.

A few pounds too many. A person unworthy of love. A scar? "Where did I . . . oh, yeah. On the playground with Larry Riordan. Playing baseball with rocks."

At odd moments, when the ego is settled, you might glimpse the miracle of life, an organic machine worthy to be called the handiwork of gods. That eye—where did such a delicate and beautiful device come from? It is mine, it is me, but I don't understand it. It is me but not as itself. It, the eye, is beyond me. Its relatives live in hawks and polar bears and millipedes. Its past is mostly unfathomable. Its future is far beyond the person looking back at you.

HOW OFTEN DO YOU CONSIDER these notions while checking for food between your teeth or straightening your hair? That image is a reminder that you exist in the eyes of others. It is what they see if they look. It's what they notice first. But it is not what you see.

If you are, like me, a black man looking for razor cuts or blemishes, do you think: *Oh, yeah. There's a black man. Not black, really, but a café au lait, milky brown. But a black man still and all. A black man whose features have been altered by East European, Native American, and other genes. A black man in the mirror. No! A black man in America. A black man in need of a shave, with a headache, a stomachache, who just received a raise?*

No. That's not what I see. The image in the mirror is a reflection of everything leading up to that moment because I am all that. It's when *you* look at me that the surface speaks.

I saw a black woman. I saw a pine tree. Same sentence structure. Shallow images. Meaningless as far as the inner life of the tree is concerned. Meaningless as far as the inner life of the woman is concerned. Could I be so empty as to consider myself a creature with only a surface? My color is part of me, like my nose. Would I say, "Hey, there's the guy with the nose in the looking glass"?

THERE'S A DIFFERENCE BETWEEN THE person we see in the mirror and those we see in the street.

My eyes are *mine,* as is my stomachache, my broken heart, my slow descent into old age.

What does this have to do with the new millennium?

Just this: We must recognize the volume and quantity of baggage that we all carry: the years of experience, the quirks of our genes. We're like tiny three-leaf weeds that have beneath us a root system larger than a peacock's fan. What we show, what we see, is nothing compared to what we are. This is why change, real change, is so difficult.

Maybe you should shed a leaf, one three-leaf weed suggests to her friend.

I've been thinking of moving out from under the shade of that big oak, yet another weed declares.

Anything is possible, but not without the knowledge of our true situation. The three-leaf weed cannot simply move out from under the shade of the all-encompassing oak. She will have to alter the excruciatingly slow process of growth to drag her leaves to a brighter sun. Failing that, she will have to scatter her seed toward the light.

We are no different. The darkness of the last few centuries is greater than the shadow of any oak tree. Our natures, language, and personal histories (both conscious and unconscious) are broader and more deeply embedded than any root system.

We have to look beyond the three leaves, the black man or white man in the street. We have to heed the image in the mirror, the glimpses of our beauty and our disappointments, the fate that is ours alone. We are not small, surface-only beings but rather vast repositories of experience and history. Just the knowledge of our language is a key to the past two thousand years of culture and history. The emotions of love or hate or fear stretch back over millions of years of evolution. The simple act of looking into a mirror and saying "That's me" represents a billion years of the striving of life.

These facets of our being are not static. They push us to act. They bind us to paths set deep in the roots of our psyches and our chromosomes.

So when one is looking toward the new millennium, she better look in the mirror. There she will see the miracle of time. There she will see the chains of her bones and the bindings of her skin. From there she might look not only at herself but at me in wonder. What an amazing creature I could become in her eyes. What hope and potential might be realized.

Then we might have a chance to join hands and move forward.

CHAPTER SIX

DEFINING THE GREAT ENEMY: THE MARGIN OF PROFIT

1.

PROGRESS IN THE WORLD TODAY is measured by increments in the margin of profit: how much you make off the labor of others,[7] off your money in the bank, off the exchange of international currency—and how much you stand to lose. We are all governed by this margin. It's like a river that we live next to, a river that gives us water and food and news from up north. It has been the aorta of human interaction in the twentieth century, and most people believe it is the only way that a nation can be great and vital.

How else can people be motivated to strive, to invent, to overcome, if not for their own profit or the profit of those closest to them? The great social experiment of Russia failed, we are told,

---

[7] The labor of your own employees or slave labor in some distant part of the globe.

because the will to achieve withered when the lazy were rewarded alongside the industrious.

It's just human nature, we hear often enough, to seek rewards for hard work and sweat. Capitalism is the natural expression of the value of labor. We were *meant* to buy and sell labor. The strong are *made* to take advantage of the weak. And we *do* take advantage. We steal and cheat and enslave. These acts keep us the strongest, if not the greatest, nation in the world.

It is certainly true that profit is a great motivator. Through PlayStation, McDonald's, various arms and aircraft dealers, Hollywood's big and little screens, and our excellently equipped armed forces, we still dominate the world's economy, culture, and hopes. When America falls down on its education, when our new crop of citizens can't add, we just import mathematicians from the former USSR and China. We can buy almost anything because almost everyone seems to want to live where he or she can be a millionaire from hard work or pure luck.

Not even *real* profit but just the slim chance, the *possibility* of a windfall, holds millions of Americans, and American wanna-bes, in thrall. It's like an obsessive psychological disease; like gambling or sex or alcohol for some. But the preoccupation with profit (the love of money, as the Christians say) is far more harmful and detrimental than having sex seven times a day or experiencing the thrill of the race. The obsession with the margin of profit grinds all that is good about us into sausage, into synthetic cases filled with an amorphous blob of meat by-products that are sold by the pound and forgotten.

Shaped like a turd or an angel, dropped out of an assembly line spout and sealed in plastic—that is our identity. Our systems are nearly perfect, but our minds are no more advanced than a dog's nose. We hanker after product and profit. Truth is not a viable asset. The cure for cancer is far less important than that ideal commodity, tobacco.

Oh, how the businessmen loved it when Mario Puzo's mobster proclaimed, "We're bigger than U.S. Steel." The margin of profit defines what is criminal and what is not. War is made reasonable by the possibility of gain (or loss). Saudi Arabia becomes a staunch ally, while Iraq, once a close friend against Iran, turns into a callow foe.

For profit we will overlook murder and rape and genocide. For profit we will accept apartheid, slavery, and even total anarchy in isolated instances. For profit we will enslave our own people. For the hope of profit a worker will mangle her mind and body doing the work of two women or three.

THE SLAVES IN AMERICA AND the serfs in Russia were freed at about the same time. The chains were laid out in front of them and the doors to the plantation were opened wide. Most slaves, most serfs, stayed on the plantation of their own accord, not because they liked it but because survival seemed reliant upon servitude.

Today the worker accepts more hours at a lower wage (or at an equal or higher wage that has lower value) or fewer hours, which mean the loss of health care and other benefits. All this for profit. When a slave is freed you can be sure that it is because she will make more profit for the plantation boss as a free agent. When a worker is lauded he's probably sweating gold.

Profit is made on a grand scale in America, but most of us don't share in it. Most of us work for dollars that fluctuate in value, at workplaces where the managers never really care about us or our hearts. We *live* within the margin of profit. We *are* the margin of profit. The money taken from our labor is used to buy political power that does not represent us. Our taxes pay for federally licensed air waves we do not control, for S&L bailouts, for public inquires into the president's privates, and for law enforcement agencies and judges who can't keep heroin out of our children's reach.

Broken roads and nonexistent stoplights, children who can't read, and prisons that are private businesses—this is also the margin, the margin of profit.[8]

The verb, then, is *marginalize*. We are marginalized by the profit of capitalism. We are footnotes to Citibank and the Mobil Oil Corporation and Chiquita Brands International (once known as the United Fruit Company). We are the edges that form the outline of the behemoth that tells us he is the only way.

God, this monster would have it, is defined by the margin of profit. We pray to him and sacrifice to him, we give our children up to him, and he's never given a single sign that he cares. This is

---

[8] The introduction of private prisons comes dangerously close to the reinstitution of slavery simply by their existence. When you add the selling of prison labor to private business you have pushed America back to a consciousness that predates the Civil War. The warden is the master and his profits rely on the labor of his inmates. And we call this nation "the land of the free."

because he *cannot* care. Labor is a commodity that is useful only as long as it is disposable. Working hands can be replaced by cheaper or more efficient labor, but if those hands can't be cut away at a moment's notice, they become a liability.

The world of profit is a world of plunder. Advancement is defined by this margin but not by the quality of life or goodness. Fair, for profit, is what you can get away with.[9] And everything is a commodity—love and hatred and the drugs you need to keep on breathing.

If profit is the only way, that is a sad state of affairs. It's a locked door, and somebody has thrown away the key.

2.

Criticizing existing political and economic systems without at least giving an idea of what can replace them is no more than idle grousing. I regret that I am not in possession of the ideal system. I don't know the exact steps that need to be taken to free us from our entanglements. Furthermore, I doubt

---

[9] And even if you get caught you still have a chance to retire young.

that it is possible for human nature to be contained within a system developed by the conscious *Homo sapiens* mind. Our passions are wider and deeper than simple structuring and decision making. Our hearts and bodies, ruled by unconscious demands moored in the history of our chromosomes, rule us more than any system or mode of production does.

Our history over the past twenty-five hundred years or so is littered with idealistic systems that have failed to free us.

Plato's *Republic* was, in part, a philosophical tirade against the failings of Athenian democracy. Plato saw a particular form of education as a rigorous system of weeding out to obtain and empower a group of enlightened rulers. These rulers would sit over the lesser population, without family ties or wealth; thus they would be relieved of the desire to pass on power or to sell it.

For Plato the state was of prime importance. Family relations and other personal freedoms were secondary.

Karl Marx believed that the economic system ruling production also ruled the social relations and political structure of nations. He believed that there was scientific necessity behind these economic forces and that there was a predictable end to social development based on the mode of production. But change, Marx declared, was necessarily accompanied by violence between the old system (represented by capitalists) and the proletariat (the workers).

Both *The Republic* and the theories of capitalism saw an enlightened dictatorship as a necessary part of the development of the state, thus exhibiting a distrust of the nature and intelligence of the common citizen. Both Platonism and Marxism were extreme ideals; both had their moments of experimentation; both failed to elate and enlighten their citizens because of their deep distrust of the minds of the masses.[10]

This distrust of human nature seems to be a valid point of view when one sees the obtuse and even criminal self-interest rampant in our nation today. A population allowed to exercise free will seems to be an open invitation to chaos.

More policemen, more prisons, more laws and audits—these seem to be the basis for peace and prosperity for the whole. Somehow these restric-

---

[10] Almost everyone is aware of the great communist revolutions of the twentieth century and of the failures that accompanied them. Plato's ideas, in one form or another, had a longer run, melding into the thousand-year-long medieval society, with its serfs and soldiers ruled over by the priesthood.

tive measures, we are told, go hand in hand with unfettered capitalism. Freedom for Americans then becomes no more than an economic issue. Money equals freedom, money equals happiness, money is even the primary element in love and beauty, royalty and intelligence. All these centuries of science and advance, and socially we are no further along than we were thousands of years ago. Actually, we may have experienced a little backsliding from some eras.

I don't think that a system can force a citizen to believe in lies. Neither can a doctrine convince the powerless of their self-determination, the poor of the basic fairness of the system of labor, or the sick that the availability of health care is not a right but a luxury.

If you don't believe in the system, then you will not treat it fairly; you will steal and condone theft, you will lose heart and choose to rebel or escape, you will hate and, in turn, become the object of hatred.

A society that puts the interests of its corporations above those of its citizens creates an untrusting and untrustworthy population. A nation where poverty is commonplace and homelessness is a reality cannot expect nationalism and self-sacrifice from the majority of its people.

What we need is a reexamination of the people and their needs. What do I give and what am I given? What do I need and what is fair for me to give back? These questions are hard to answer because of the spectacles and illusions I mentioned earlier and because the margin of profit has different notions of need than does its constituent labor force. The margin of profit needs us fed enough and healthy enough to work—at the lowest possible cost. The lion's share of the profit is fed back into the process of capital. Better machines, faster processes, and more efficient exploitation of natural resources and the labor force are the goals of capitalism. A happier, longer, healthier life are the goals of the worker, a better world, a bright future for the children, the faith that one can survive without destroying one's neighbors.

There's a natural conflict between the Lilliputian population of workers and the humongous beast of production. We, the workers, support this great system upon its mighty pedestal at the top of the world. Some orts trickle down to us, but only enough to keep us working, only enough to help us strain and push the burden of capital higher. Our individual strengths, our communal strengths, belong to the task of corporate America; subsequently, the task of corporate America gains weight and velocity. All of this can be understood in relation to the margin of profit. The greater the profit, the less we make. The less we make, the more we have to work.[11] The more we work, the more we are restricted by the chain of our labors.

I'D LIKE TO SAY THAT the answer to the problem is the simple abandonment of the economic system that rules us. We should all work together, we should all live well. Give our all and share in the wealth; it's a beautiful notion, and maybe our children's children will have learned enough to make such a world work. But we, like the slaves of the nineteenth century, have been conditioned to

---

[11] I like to explain the equation by looking back toward the middle of the twentieth century. At that time, for middle America, the one-job household was common. Often one worker made enough for food, the mortgage, the Christmas club, the college fund, and the ten-dollar doctor and dentist visits. Today that worker makes many more dollars, but the one-job household is a thing of the past. The expenses of life have risen much more quickly than the increases in salary. Both parents have to work now. Three kids in good colleges is a fortune that few pocketbooks can bear.

imprisonment defined by the alienation of our labor: We give 100 percent and receive somewhat less in return. We take what we are given and make what we can of it between the demands placed upon us for the privilege of freedom.

Fine. For the moment, let's accept the system. Let's agree that the corporate, capitalist, alienated form of labor is what we have to work with. Still, can't we make a few demands? Can't we ask a few questions about ourselves on the coffee break and during commercials?

The margin of profit, among other things, defines our labor; more, it defines our humanity. The job you hold, the income you bring home, the recognition of your value to society, are all deeply informed by your labors. And if the system defines you, then it owes you something too. The question is, what are you owed?

This question must be articulated and answered by at least 10 percent of the population. Ten percent is an arbitrary number. I'm simply saying that the number of people that it takes to make political change is actually quite small. A fraction of the populace that is sure of what changes are necessary can change the minds of their neighbors. Truth (as mentioned in the earlier section) comes in small packages. During the twelve weeks of abstinence from arena sports and electronic media you could ask yourself what it is that you deserve for a lifetime of labor. Make a list. Share it with whoever will listen.

Maybe you think that a medical bill of rights makes sense. Maybe you think that every American child deserves an excellent education. Maybe you believe that the child-bearing *job*, not yet a property of capitalism, should be remunerated and revered by the state. Write it down and spread it around.

Maybe we need more doctors and scientists, and maybe the output from these laborers should be the communal property of the people. Maybe the margin of profit that works for cornflakes should be monitored more closely when it comes to medicine and war. Maybe profit and medicine don't mix.

Maybe you need a place to sleep and you won't sleep soundly until you know that everyone is safe and sound here in the bosom of the richest nation in the history of the world.

Make a list; put it in your wallet. Take it out now and then to tinker with it or expand it. Make decisions based on this list. Vote by it and argue for its claims. Compare the ideas of your bosses and political leaders with what you think is right. Then make another list, this time of those people and systems that support your notions. Notice who and what is missing from this list.

The goals of revolution are realized by personal enlightenment. Don't buy somebody else's list; don't clip one from the newspaper. It's not in Mao's "little red book" or in the Declaration of Independence either. Any life that you can attain must be, in part, the production of your own mind. What you need is missing from your life right now. Reach out for it. Define it. Then demand it from the world.

This simple exercise is nothing new, I know. I am not trying to innovate. Innovation, when it comes to a population in the billions, can easily lead to mass murder.[12] I'm simply trying to lay a few notions next to each other: the margin of profit to the right, a list of my demands to the left. The TV is off, the election is next year, it's evening, and, like Sisyphus, I have a few moments before I have to continue the labors forced upon me by the gods.

---

[12] From Germany to the USSR, from China to Cambodia to Guatemala, we see the logical end to philosophy and politics to be genocide. America's own native population fell to the new ways of the white world.

Once you throw your chip into the game, the odds are changed, the revolution of enlightenment gains, and the margin of profit quavers toward a counter move.

I WANT TO UNDERSCORE THE power I see in these pedestrian suggestions for change. The economic system we live in needs our approbation; it needs us to agree that things are the way they should be. If the people's attitude toward the system breaks away from the lassitude brought on by spectacles and illusion, if our commitments to our own needs and our own natures outstrip the fear we have from the consequences presented by capitalism—then the giant defined by profit will have to alter its strategy toward us. And if, like the courageous slave mentioned above, we also refuse to see others enslaved just as much as we refuse to wear the yoke of production—then the system of production may have met its match; then we shall be served by the product of our labors rather than serving the system of production.

The idealism of this logic is obvious but to

have ideals, to believe in what is right, is a part of human nature—it is why we have survived this long. We should follow our natures, our beliefs. That way, even in failure, we have lived up to our human potentials.

CHAPTER SEVEN

My Platform for the Presidency

1.

M ANY WILL ARGUE WITH MY notion that it
is the chains forged in the twentieth century, and not free will, that predict our future.
They might say, "Look at America. See freedom at
work. It's not chains that define us but rather human rights and the right of free elections."

One man, one vote. That's what they say.

But what do we vote for? Is that vote enough
to make us free? Voting for one white man in a
suit over another white man in a suit? There are
no Jews or Hispanics, American Indians or Viet-
namese up there in the presidential arena. No
black people either. No women. If there's a ho-
mosexual up there, he'd better keep it hidden.

The guy hoping to lead us all is probably mar-
ried, definitely Christian, and with a college degree
in something like law or history or political science.
The camera has to like this candidate. And he has

to be well versed in the machinery of one of two political parties. Also, he must be well spoken in the politically acceptable expressions of racism, sexism, and equal rights. He can't be too young, but great age is also a detriment.

The man who takes our vote can't want to rock the boat too much. He needs to be good at hiding his heterosexuality when it applies to anyone outside of the institution of his prescribed marriage.

He is, in short, a figurehead, a man who is like the black man someone saw go into Joe's house, an image of a man that holds no surprises. A man who not only upholds the status quo but who is himself that status quo. He is what most of us are not, but still he is the only choice that we have to vote for.

What kind of freedom is that? More like a game show with contestants than a serious encounter between real-life candidates. Or maybe a beauty pageant with everything but the bathing suit competition.

What kind of democracy gives you two candidates who represent less than 5 percent of the population? What kind of choice is that?

My problem with the process of democracy in America is twofold. The first part has to do with how the candidates get out before the people. The second is who those candidates *are* for us. The answers to these questions are intricately intertwined.

Money puts candidates on the ballot, on the TV screen, on the walls all around the town, and finally in the seat of power. Money, that foulest drug of the modern world, uses its addictive powers to bind even our exercise of the democratic process. From John Kennedy to Ronald Reagan, it's cold cash that fuels the passions of democracy.

Wealth buys the presidency. Wealth is the most important political constituent. And so we are saddled with representatives who mind (and mine) the interests of corporations and millionaires. We therefore have a two-tiered legal system, one for the rich and another for the poor. As a result, most Americans, citizens of the richest and most technologically advanced country in the history of the world, find themselves voting to keep the flow of crumbs from stopping. We vote for the right to work until we are too old for anything else anymore.

And as wealth buys the presidency, it also buys the president. The candidate, the elected official, must tend to the true constituency, money. Therefore issues of race, gender, age, sexuality, and any other surface difference lose meaning. It's money that rules the political arena.

Our political system is a travesty. The health care we are provided with, the retirement plan the government forces us to participate in, and the pollution of our dreams for a future worth living all serve to limit the everyday person, to chain her to a life of grunting lies.

2.

"Yes, yes, yes," you say. "The government is bad and my elected officials are corrupt. What do you want me to do about it? Human political organization has always had this kind of corruption. That's just the way things are. Don't complain to me, *do* something."

This is a good argument. Changing the way things are is the only way to make the world a better place. This doesn't mean a violent revolution resulting in fifty years of eating potatoes with no salt. No. The power of change is within our grasp by peaceful and legal means.

The right to vote is good. Voting for what you really want and for what you really believe is perfection. But in order to vote for your own benefit you must first articulate your desires, your perfect world.

When you sit down in a room alone and begin to think of your perfect world, though, you will most likely run into a new set of chains: the chains of apathy.

As life has gone on, your expectations have probably eroded. Your dreams for new worlds and adventure have faded to plans for two or three weeks of vacation. Your deepest childhood desires seem funny to you, even though they still have a place in your heart. The workaday world has set limits on us all. *How can I change the world when I can't even get a raise? How can I exercise free will when my boss tells me when I can go to lunch and how long I have to eat?*

If you ask most Americans what they do, how many will include in their reply, "I exercise my rights as a citizen by voting"? Not many, I believe. Apathy has set in like arthritis. It limits our emotional movements and dampens our intellectual ardor. These chains, once they are in place, seem to be a just punishment, because, after all, look at us: we're barely able to keep up.

But it's not true. The chains of apathy come from the way we have all been compartmentalized in our daily labors. Human beings are social creatures (or at least partly so). Through the eons we have relied on each other to help raise children, to build shelter, and to search for food. Survival of the individual and survival of the group were synonymous. There were, of course, economic relations from early on in human development. But these relations were not systematized to the level ushered in by the Industrial Revolution. Personal and community economics, no matter their shortcomings, necessarily included the individual members by name. But today each individual has a number and a relationship to his or her employer. If I want child care or education or shelter, I have to buy it. I have sole responsibility even when the costs are too high. I can never rest or contemplate or feel part of the larger whole.

These are attributes of slavery.

No, you're right, you are not a slave. You are free, free to starve unless you strive in the ways allowed by the boss.

THE ONLY WAY OUT IS to be crazy, to imagine the impossible and the ridiculous, to say what it is that you want in spite of everyone else's embarrassed laughs. This is a little easier for me because I am a fiction writer. Pushing ideas to their limits is what I'm expected to do—*in fiction*. But it's a small skip from fiction to nonfiction in this world of technology and change.

And so to my candidacy.

My platform has two parts: immediate concerns and plans for the future.

As far as immediate concerns go, I believe that we should assure the education of our children and the welfare of our aged—children because they are our only real natural resource, and the aged because they built the world you see outside your window every day. I think the government needs to insure doctors against liability and that we need to dramatically increase the number of doctors and health care professionals. We should either legalize drugs or stop the flow of these narcotics across our borders. I say that if the government is unable, or unwilling, to end this traffic, then we should decriminalize the product, therefore decriminalizing a large portion of our population.

We also need to have a constitutional conference on capital punishment.[13]

---

[13] The halls of death rows across the nation are filled mostly with nonwhite and poor white men. There is an injustice in this fact. Either sentence all capital crimes with the same murderous zeal or outlaw the persecution of our poor and minorities.

As far as affirmative action goes—I'm for it, just not in its current form. Affirmative action, for me, means that everyone has a right to a living wage, a right to competent medical care, and a share in the natural resources that the nation either owns or creates. Everybody has the right to a good life. No one will be excluded.

There's nothing easy about getting the good life. The margin of profit has to be extended to cover these assurances to the working population. These goals contradict the notion of capitalism and the competition of the international labor force. Capping salaries, *conserving* resources, and privatizing everything from transportation to prisons is the trend.

In order to attain the above goals we will have to forge a new foreign policy that works out with our economic allies a code for the international right to the good life. We must limit rampant competition among international corporations by making accords for international workers' rights.

That's it for my immediate campaign. Now for plans for the future.

It seems to me that the desires of most people concern safety and a long life. These, then, are my campaign promises. I will work to bend the power of this nation toward the goals of extending life, eliminating the age factor from human cells,[14] designing cities and living spaces that are optimal for human comfort and safety, and preparing us psychologically for such tremendous changes in our expectations of life.

Ridiculous, wouldn't you say?

Not as ridiculous as a poor community trying, and failing, to get a stoplight installed so that children will be safe from careening cars. Not as ridiculous as a nation with the largest, best-equipped army in the world still being unable to stop the flow of drugs on the street. Not as ridiculous as the atomic bomb or Star Wars or germ warfare. Not as ridiculous as the trillions of dollars we spend on automobiles and gasoline instead of efficient public transportation. Not as ridiculous as a construction worker who spent his whole life building but who ends his days with no roof over his head. Not as ridiculous as children living in poverty. Not as ridiculous as the billions of commercial dollars spent reporting on O.J. Simpson and Monica Lewinsky.

---

[14] This, of course, will raise the ugly specter of overpopulation, but the technological war to create space sounds better than Star Wars to me.

Eternal youth and a good place to spend it sound eminently sane to me. I don't need a Kennedy or a Clinton or a Reagan. I don't need a political party to realize my goals. We are on the verge of technological progress that will rip asunder these petty nineteenth-century systems that we embrace as if they were religion. Desiring comfort is not a race thing, a gender thing, a class thing.

Most voters don't really care about a pretty face, but you better believe they'd turn out for the cure for cancer; they'd be casting their votes for an extra ten years of life.

My candidacy is based on my desire to break the chains of yesterday's politics. Cigar-smoking Republicans and racist Democrats—I don't need them. What I want is freedom to share in the incredible wealth of our minds. Let's build a world where progress is for everyone and ownership is for us all. I'm not talking about material ownership here. What I'm saying is that our citizens should have equal access to the advantages that we discover. Medical care, education, a living wage, and peace of mind should be available for everyone.

READING BACK OVER THESE WORDS, I see that I've crossed over from idealism to utopian thought. I'm asking for a perfect world in the face of the stark realism of multinational corporate competition (war against the poor instead of a war on poverty). And as much as I said earlier that we have to accept sounding ridiculous if we want change, I still find myself shy, desiring to delete this section of my essay.

I want to hide from this embarrassment because I know that there is no candidate with the power to change the direction of American political forces. I know that voting once every four years and waiting to see what happens is more a lesson in futility than an exercise of democracy.

The president, the alderman, the senator, and the county sheriff all have the same problems when it comes to occupying office. They need money and a constituency that will support their actions. They need to make deals and listen to the people who wield the real power—the political bosses. They need room to move within the framework of lies generated by the media, political interest groups, and corporate systems of information.

A single vote is a given thing, a Democratic or Republican thing, a ticket that is worthless unless you turn it in at the door. And the show you see is not the spontaneous performance you expected. The show was worked out a long time ago, and you and I are just playing our roles.

In order to change things you need a wild-card candidate, one with a crazy platform such as the one I put forward here. But you also need a deeper knowledge of, and a deeper still commitment to, the democratic process. You need to attend meetings, send letters, form together into groups and approach your congressional representatives. You need to take time away from the TV and the sitcoms. You need to talk at work and at mothers' meetings. You need to treat the democratic process as a revolution of ideas, as if America is being formed and reformed every four years.

A leader can't lead those who have given up hope. A leader can't lead a people who are stagnating, who are following the program.

Maybe we can have wild dreams that are beyond what we have been told is possible. Maybe our labor and our citizenship are more closely aligned than we think.

Reading a few books, writing a few letters, and talking a few hours each week might prove more valuable than a fifteen-hundred-dollar lotto jackpot or a raise or retirement one day.

The nation and its potentials are ours to command. Imagine that. *Ours to command.* Maybe the way things are isn't the way they have to be. Maybe we could be on the move.

How many hours would it take? Two for researching a particular issue each week. Two hours to talk to a group of five friends once a week. Thirty minutes for phone calls to your political representatives. Thirty minutes to write letters to the people who make decisions. One person doing it would be like a raindrop on a sunny day. But three hundred million people, even if they were, in many respects, opposed at first, would be a storm on our capitols. And the dialogues raised would change the world.

You have the vote again in this year, 2000, and then in 2004. If you vote the party ticket and then wait in front of your TV for the next four years, remember: The millennium passed but nothing changed. You're still wearing the chains that your grandparents forged at the behest of the company store.

CHAPTER EIGHT

LAST WORDS

"YOU HAVE BEEN BAMBOOZLED," SAID Malcolm X to his followers in Harlem. And he was right. Black people had been fooled and lied to and broken over the promise of freedom. But the truth is that all Americans have been fooled and broken.

Democracy and capitalism make strange bedfellows. In this odd brew freedom becomes a commodity. A price is put upon our only asset, our labor. The right to decide, about anything, seems to have been taken out of our hands. But still we have the right to cast ballots. We still have the right to make decisions, even though the choices we are given would seem to deny that fact.

This brief and inadequate essay has tried to make hints about how we can see around the bright lights meant to blind us to the choices we have—first to recognize some of the restraints placed on us by the organization of labor and popular culture, then to see, from a calm place, that there might be a world in our hearts that we would like to realize, first by speaking out, then by shouting out, and finally by action.

I would also hope that I have given some reason for blacks and whites, and all the other cultures and races, to look to each other's histories as guideposts and warnings, to see that we are really in the same boat, that if the boat sinks we all go down.

Finally I hope that I have addressed the notion of the passage of time. Time passing by itself means nothing. In order to celebrate a new age we must create a new age. And creation is the hardest trick of all.

INDEX

ABOUT THE AUTHOR

WALTER MOSLEY is the bestselling author of many works, including five critically acclaimed mysteries featuring Easy Rawlins—*Devil in a Blue Dress*, the first book in that series, was later made into a feature film produced by Jonathan Demme; the blues novel *RL's Dream*, which was a finalist for the NAACP Award in Fiction and winner of the Black Caucus of the American Library Association's Literary Award; the story collection *Always Outnumbered, Always Outgunned*, which received the Anisfield-Wolf Book Award; and the science fiction novel *Blue Light*, a national bestseller.

In 1966 Mosley was named the first Artist-in-Residence at New York University's Africana Studies Institute. Since that residency, he has continued to work with the department, creating an innovative lecture series entitled "Black Genius," which will bring diverse speakers from art, politics, and academe to discuss practical solutions to contemporary issues. Designed as a "public classroom," these lectures will include speakers ranging from Spike Lee to Angela Davis. The speeches from this program were recently published in the collection *Black Genius*.

Mosley founded PEN American Center's Open

Book Committee, which sought to increase the presence of minorities in the publishing industry. He has also created at CUNY a new publishing certificate program aimed at young urban residents. Mosley also serves on the board of directors of the National Book Awards, the Poetry Society of America, and Manhattan Theatre Club and is the past president of the Mystery Writers of America.

Mosley is the winner of the TransAfrica International Literary Prize. His books have been translated into twenty languages. He lives in New York.

A Note on The Library of Contemporary Thought

This exciting new series tackles today's most provocative, fascinating, and relevant issues, giving top opinion makers a forum to explore topics that matter urgently to themselves and their readers. Some will be think pieces. Some will be research oriented. Some will be journalistic in nature. The form is wide open, but the aim is the same: to say things that need saying.